DEFI
FOR BEGINNERS

A COMPREHENSIVE GUIDE TO GETTING STARTED
EVERYTHING YOU NEED TO KNOW

DONATELLO JAMES

CONTENTS

ABOUT THE AUTHOR

Allow me to introduce myself—I am Donatello, a dedicated and passionate expert in the world of Decentralized Finance, affectionately known as DeFi. My journey into this exhilarating realm has been a combination of hands-on experience and intensive boot camp studies under the guidance of true DeFi leaders. As you dive into the pages of this book, I want you to know that my mission is to share the wealth of knowledge I've accumulated with the global DeFi community and the broader mainstream audience.

My fascination with DeFi began when I ventured into the field armed with nothing but curiosity and an eager appetite for learning. Through countless hours of research, experimentation, and real-world experiences, I witnessed firsthand the transformative power of decentralized finance. The decentralized nature of DeFi opens doors to financial inclusivity, transparency, and innovation that were previously unimaginable. It's a world where traditional financial intermediaries take a backseat, and individuals like you and me can take control of our financial destinies.

My education in DeFi was not limited to theoretical concepts and academic teachings alone. I immersed myself in the vibrant DeFi ecosystem, collaborating with experts already making waves in the field. These mentors and collaborators generously shared their wisdom, helping me grasp the complexities of this evolving landscape. Their insights, combined with my own experiences, form the foundation of the knowledge I'm excited to impart to you.

Through this book, I aim to simplify DeFi, breaking down complex concepts into digestible pieces, and offering practical guidance for both beginners and experienced enthusiasts. Whether you're here to gain a basic understanding of DeFi or to dive deeper into advanced, I'm committed to providing you with the tools and insights you need to navigate this dynamic and sometimes challenging space.

Join me on this thrilling journey through the world of DeFi. Together, we will explore the myriad possibilities, potential pitfalls, and exciting innovations that await those who dare to venture into this decentralized frontier. My hope is that, by the time you finish reading these pages, you will be equipped not only with knowledge but also with the confidence to participate actively in the ever-evolving world of DeFi.

Thank you for joining me on this exciting adventure. Let's Begin!

INTRODUCTION TO DEFI: THE POWER OF DECENTRALIZED FINANCE

Welcome to the world of DeFi, where traditional finance meets the innovative potential of blockchain technology. In recent years, a new paradigm has emerged, challenging the conventional financial systems that have long been entrenched in centralized control. DeFi, short for Decentralized Finance, represents a transformative shift towards a more open, inclusive, and transparent financial ecosystem.

Imagine a world where financial services are not solely controlled by banks or intermediaries but are accessible to anyone with an internet connection. A world where transactions can be conducted securely, instantly, and without the need for trust in a central authority. This is the promise that DeFi holds, and it is reshaping the way we think about money, investments, business and the future of finance.

At its core, DeFi is built upon the principles of decentralization, transparency, and open access. It leverages blockchain technology, primarily the EVM blockchains with Etheruem leading the way, to create a global financial infrastructure that operates without the limitations and inefficiencies of traditional systems. By utilizing smart contracts, which are self-executing agreements running on the blockchain, DeFi enables the automation and execution of financial transactions and contracts in a secure and tamper-proof manner.

In this book, we will embark on a journey to demystify DeFi and provide you with the knowledge and tools to navigate this exciting and rapidly evolving landscape. Whether you are a beginner eager to understand the fundamentals or an experienced enthusiast seeking to expand your expertise, this book aims to be your comprehensive guide.

We will start by exploring the core principles that underpin DeFi, diving into concepts such as decentralization, transparency, and permissionless innovation. Understanding these principles will lay the groundwork for comprehending the unique benefits and advantages that DeFi offers to individuals worldwide.

As we progress, we will delve into the key components of DeFi, including smart contracts, decentralized exchanges, stablecoins, lending and borrowing protocols, and yield farming. Through clear explanations and real-world examples, you will gain a solid understanding of how each of these components contributes to the broader DeFi ecosystem.

We will also address the risks and challenges inherent in DeFi and discuss strategies for mitigating them. While the potential for high returns and financial freedom is present, it is crucial to approach DeFi with caution and awareness of the associated risks. By equipping yourself with knowledge, you can make informed decisions and navigate this dynamic landscape more confidently.

Practical guidance is a vital aspect of this book. We will provide step-by-step instructions on how to get started with DeFi, from setting up a digital wallet to choosing reliable platforms and implementing security best practices. Whether you are new to cryptocurrencies or have been a long-time participant in the crypto space, this book aims to support you in taking your first steps or expanding your horizons in DeFi.

Moreover, we will explore various DeFi use cases that are accessible to individuals at different levels of experience. From decentralized lending and borrowing to automated market making, yield farming, and liquidity provision, we will examine how these applications function and the potential benefits they offer.

To cater to readers with a deeper interest in the subject, we will touch upon advanced DeFi concepts such as layer 2 scaling solutions, interoperability, cross-chain protocols, and decentralized autonomous organizations (DAOs). These advanced topics provide a glimpse into the cutting-edge developments and future possibilities within the DeFi ecosystem.

Throughout this book, we will highlight current trends shaping DeFi and provide insights into the future outlook of decentralized finance. By staying informed and understanding the evolving landscape, you will be better equipped to adapt and seize the opportunities that arise.

So, whether you are a curious individual seeking financial empowerment, an investor looking for new avenues of growth, or a technologist passionate about the potential of blockchain, this book is here to empower you. Together, let's unlock the power of decentralized finance and embrace the future of financial innovation.

UNDERSTANDING THE CORE PRINCIPLES OF DEFI: DECENTRALIZATION, TRANSPARENCY, AND PERMISSIONLESS INNOVATION

At the heart of the DeFi revolution lie three core principles: decentralization, transparency, and permissionless innovation. These principles are the pillars upon which the entire DeFi ecosystem is built, reshaping the traditional financial landscape and creating new opportunities for individuals across the globe.

Decentralization:

DeFi embraces the concept of decentralization, which means that financial activities and decision-making are not controlled by a central authority or intermediary. Instead, they are executed on decentralized networks, primarily leveraging blockchain technology. By removing the need for intermediaries such as banks or brokers and governments. DeFi aims to empower individuals, allowing them to have direct control over their financial assets and transactions. Decentralization fosters trust, as transactions and agreements are governed by smart contracts that automatically execute predefined conditions, without relying on a single entity.

Transparency:

Transparency is a fundamental aspect of DeFi. Unlike traditional financial systems where transactions and processes are often opaque, DeFi promotes transparency through the use of public blockchains. Every transaction and interaction is recorded on the blockchain, visible to anyone who cares to explore the network. This transparency not only ensures accountability but also enables users to verify the integrity and authenticity of transactions. It promotes trust among participants and allows for a more open and auditable financial system.

Permissionless Innovation:

One of the most exciting aspects of DeFi is the principle of permissionless innovation. It means that anyone with an internet connection and the necessary tools can participate in the DeFi ecosystem. There are no gatekeepers or restrictive barriers to entry. This openness encourages individuals to create, experiment, and contribute to the development of new

3

financial applications and services. As a result, the DeFi space is witnessing rapid innovation, with new protocols, platforms, and financial instruments being introduced regularly. Permissionless innovation empowers individuals to shape the future of finance and business, bringing forth novel solutions and challenging traditional financial and business models.

These core principles of decentralization, transparency, and permissionless innovation are interdependent and synergistic. They work together to create a more inclusive and equitable financial system that is accessible to anyone, regardless of their background or geographical location. By adhering to these principles, DeFi aims to address the limitations and inefficiencies of centralized finance, promoting financial autonomy, privacy, and opportunities for individuals globally.

It is important to note that while these principles drive the DeFi movement, they also come with unique challenges and considerations. The decentralized nature of DeFi can make it susceptible to security risks, such as smart contract vulnerabilities or hacking attempts. The transparency of the blockchain means that transactions, once recorded, are immutable, which requires users to exercise caution and conduct thorough due diligence. Additionally, the permissionless nature of innovation may lead to a crowded and competitive market, making it crucial for participants to stay informed and make informed choices.

As we navigate the world of DeFi, understanding and embracing these core principles will guide our interactions and decisions. By recognizing the power of decentralization, the value of transparency, and the potential of permissionless innovation, we can harness the transformative potential of DeFi to build a more inclusive and resilient financial ecosystem.

SMART CONTRACTS: THE FOUNDATION OF DEFI

At the core of the DeFi ecosystem lies one of its most powerful and revolutionary components: smart contracts. Smart contracts are self-executing agreements written in code that automatically execute predefined conditions when specific criteria are met. They serve as the building blocks of decentralized finance, enabling a wide range of financial and contract activities to be performed with trust, security, and transparency.

What are Smart Contracts?

Smart contracts are computer programs that run on blockchain networks, most commonly on EVM blockchains with Ethereum leading the way. They are designed to facilitate, verify, and enforce the negotiation or performance of agreements between parties without the need for intermediaries. These contracts are written in programming languages, with the most common language being solidity, specifically tailored for the blockchain environment.

Autonomy and Trustlessness:

Smart contracts introduce a new level of autonomy and trustlessness to financial transactions. By eliminating the need for intermediaries or centralized authorities, individuals can directly interact with smart contracts, reducing reliance on third parties. The predefined conditions and rules embedded in the contract ensure that the execution of transactions is automatic and immutable once triggered, minimizing the potential for fraud or manipulation.

Secure and Immutable Execution:

One of the key advantages of smart contracts is their secure and immutable execution. Once deployed on the blockchain, smart contracts cannot be modified or tampered with, providing a high level of security and eliminating the risk of unauthorized alterations. This immutability ensures that the terms of the contract, including the distribution of funds or certain conditions, are executed exactly as programmed, without the possibility of interference.

Programmable Money and Financial Logic:

Smart contracts enable the creation of programmable money and financial logic, revolutionizing traditional financial instruments and processes. They can represent a wide range of financial agreements, such as loans, insurance policies, decentralized exchanges, yield farming protocols, savings and more. The flexibility and programmability of smart contracts allow for the automation and customization of financial operations, creating new opportunities and possibilities.

Interoperability and Composability:

Smart contracts in DeFi are designed to be interoperable and composable. This means that they can interact and integrate with other smart contracts and DeFi protocols, forming a complex and interconnected ecosystem. This composability enables the building of sophisticated financial applications and allows for the seamless movement of assets and liquidity across different platforms and services.

Open Source and Community-driven Development:

Smart contracts in DeFi are often open source, meaning their code is publicly available for scrutiny and improvement by the community. This transparency fosters collaboration, peer review, and the identification and resolution of vulnerabilities or bugs. The community-driven development of smart contracts encourages innovation, ensures continuous improvement, and enhances the security and reliability of the DeFi ecosystem.

Smart contracts are the backbone of DeFi, enabling a myriad of financial, personal and business activities in a decentralized and transparent manner. By utilizing these programmable agreements, individuals can interact with various DeFi protocols, participate in lending and borrowing, trade digital assets, stake tokens, and much more, all without the need for intermediaries or centralized control. The power of smart contracts has opened up a new world of possibilities, revolutionizing the financial, business and personal landscape, empowering individuals to take control of their financial lives.

DECENTRALIZED EXCHANGES: EMPOWERING PEER-TO-PEER TRADING IN DEFI

Decentralized exchanges (DEXs) play a pivotal role in the DeFi ecosystem by providing a platform for individuals to trade digital assets in a peer-to-peer manner. Unlike traditional centralized exchanges, DEXs operate without intermediaries, giving users direct control over their funds and fostering greater transparency and security. Let's explore the key components and functionalities of decentralized exchanges.

Peer-to-Peer Trading:

Decentralized exchanges enable users to trade digital assets directly with one another, removing the need for intermediaries such as brokers or centralized order books. Through the use of smart contracts, DEXs facilitate trustless transactions, where assets are swapped directly between users' wallets without relying on a central authority.

Non-Custodial Nature:

One of the distinguishing features of DEXs is their non-custodial nature. Unlike centralized exchanges that require users to deposit their funds into a centralized wallet, DEXs allow users to retain control over their assets throughout the trading process. Users' funds remain in their wallets until a trade is executed, reducing the risk of hacks or theft associated with centralized custodial exchanges.

Order Books and Automated Market Making:

Decentralized exchanges employ different mechanisms for facilitating trades. Some DEXs use order books similar to traditional exchanges, where users can place buy or sell orders at specified prices. Others utilize automated market making (AMM) models, often powered by liquidity pools, which automatically match buy and sell orders based on predefined algorithms. AMMs provide liquidity and allow users to trade assets instantly, even for less liquid tokens.

Liquidity Pools and Token Swapping:

Liquidity pools are integral to the functioning of many decentralized exchanges. Users can contribute their assets to these pools, which serve as reservoirs of liquidity for various trading pairs. Liquidity providers are incentivized through earning fees generated by trades in proportion to their contribution. This enables users to easily swap between different tokens without relying on a counterparty, as the liquidity pools provide the necessary liquidity for trades.

Interoperability and Cross-Chain Trading:

Some DEXs have implemented cross-chain functionality, enabling users to trade assets across different blockchain networks. This interoperability expands the reach and liquidity of decentralized exchanges, allowing for seamless trading between tokens on different blockchains. Cross-chain DEXs utilize technologies like changenow or bridge protocols to facilitate trustless token transfers between blockchains.

Governance Tokens and Decentralized Governance:

Many decentralized exchanges incorporate governance tokens into their ecosystem. These tokens grant holders certain rights, such as voting on protocol upgrades, fee distributions, or other important decisions related to the platform. Governance tokens encourage community participation and give users a voice in shaping the future of the DEX.

Decentralized exchanges form a critical infrastructure within the DeFi ecosystem, enabling individuals to trade digital assets in a peer-to-peer, non-custodial, and transparent manner. By leveraging smart contracts, liquidity pools, and innovative trading models, DEXs empower users with greater control over their assets while facilitating efficient and secure trading experiences. As the DeFi space continues to evolve, decentralized exchanges are poised to play an even more significant role, providing liquidity, expanding market access, and driving the future of decentralized finance.

STABLECOINS: STABILITY AND ACCESSIBILITY IN THE DEFI ECOSYSTEM

Stablecoins are a vital component of the DeFi ecosystem, serving as digital assets designed to maintain a stable value, typically pegged to a reserve asset like fiat currency or commodities. These stable digital currencies provide stability, liquidity, and accessibility to the decentralized finance space. Let's explore the key components and functionalities of stablecoins in DeFi.

Stability:

The primary characteristic of stablecoins is their stability. Unlike volatile cryptocurrencies such as Bitcoin or Ethereum, stablecoins aim to maintain a relatively fixed value, often pegged to a stable asset like the US dollar (USD) or another fiat currency. Stablecoins achieve stability through various mechanisms, including collateralization, algorithmic algorithms, or a combination of both.

Collateralization:

Many stablecoins are collateralized, meaning they are backed by reserve assets held in a custodial or decentralized manner. These assets provide the necessary collateral to support the stablecoin's value and maintain stability. Common collateral types include fiat currencies, cryptocurrencies, or even other stablecoins. Collateralization ensures that stablecoins maintain their pegged value by allowing users to redeem or exchange them for the underlying assets, creating trust and stability.

Algorithmic Stability:

Some stablecoins, known as algorithmic stablecoins, do not rely on traditional collateralization but instead use algorithms and smart contracts to maintain their stability. These stablecoins adjust their supply dynamically based on market demand and supply conditions. Through various mechanisms, such as expanding or contracting the token supply or implementing stabilization mechanisms like algorithmic bonding curves, algorithmic stablecoins aim to stabilize their value without relying on physical reserves.

Liquidity and Accessibility:

Stablecoins provide liquidity and accessibility within the DeFi ecosystem. They serve as an essential medium of exchange, enabling users to move value quickly and efficiently within decentralized applications, decentralized exchanges (DEXs), and other financial protocols. Stablecoins also offer an on-ramp and off-ramp for users to easily transition between traditional financial systems and the DeFi space, as they provide a familiar and stable unit of value.

Programmability and Integration:

Stablecoins, like other cryptocurrencies, benefit from the programmability of blockchain technology. They can be seamlessly integrated into various DeFi protocols, allowing for programmable money and sophisticated financial operations. Stablecoins can be used for lending and borrowing, decentralized trading, yield farming, remittances, and more. Their programmability opens up a wide range of possibilities, making stablecoins a versatile tool for decentralized financial applications.

Transparency and Auditability:

Stablecoins built on public blockchains provide transparency and auditability. Transactions and holdings can be tracked on the blockchain, ensuring that the stablecoin is adequately collateralized and maintaining trust among users. Public blockchains enable real-time verification and allow users to monitor the stablecoin's pegged value and the underlying collateral, providing an additional layer of confidence.

Stablecoins serve as a cornerstone of DeFi, offering stability, liquidity, and accessibility to users within the decentralized finance ecosystem. By providing a reliable medium of exchange and store of value, stablecoins enable seamless transactions and bridge the gap between traditional financial systems and the decentralized world. As the DeFi landscape continues to evolve, stablecoins will continue to play a crucial role in enabling decentralized financial services and unlocking the potential for a more inclusive and borderless financial future.

LENDING AND BORROWING PROTOCOLS: ENABLING DEFI CREDIT MARKETS

Lending and borrowing protocols form a vital component of the DeFi ecosystem, providing individuals with the ability to access credit, earn interest on their assets, and facilitate peer-to-peer lending without the need for traditional financial intermediaries. These protocols leverage the power of smart contracts and blockchain technology to create efficient and transparent credit markets within the decentralized finance space. Let's explore the key components and functionalities of lending and borrowing protocols in DeFi.

Peer-to-Peer Lending:

DeFi lending protocols enable individuals to lend and borrow directly from one another in a peer-to-peer manner. Smart contracts govern the lending and borrowing process, automatically executing agreements based on predefined terms and conditions. By removing intermediaries, DeFi lending protocols allow for greater accessibility, efficiency, and potentially lower interest rates compared to traditional lending systems.

Collateralized Loans:

Collateralized loans are a prevalent feature in DeFi lending protocols. Borrowers can provide digital assets as collateral to secure a loan, ensuring that lenders have recourse in the event of default. Collateralization mitigates the risk associated with lending and allows borrowers to access credit based on the value of their existing assets. Smart contracts lock the collateral, and in the event of default, lenders can liquidate the collateral to recover their funds.

Overcollateralization and Loan-to-Value (LTV) Ratios:

To maintain the stability of the lending market, many DeFi lending protocols require borrowers to overcollateralize their loans. Overcollateralization involves providing more collateral than the borrowed amount, creating a cushion to protect lenders from potential price volatility or default risk. Loan-to-Value (LTV) ratios define the maximum loan amount that borrowers can obtain based on the value of the collateral. LTV ratios ensure that the collateral value is sufficient to cover the loan, maintaining the security of the lending protocol.

Interest Rates and Yield Generation:

DeFi lending protocols allow users to earn interest on their assets by lending them to borrowers. The interest rates are typically determined by supply and demand dynamics within the lending market and can vary based on factors such as the availability of assets and market conditions. Lenders earn interest on their deposited assets, providing an opportunity for passive income generation. Borrowers, in turn, pay interest on the funds they borrow, facilitating access to credit within the DeFi ecosystem.

Liquidity Pools and Automated Market Making:

Some lending protocols utilize liquidity pools and automated market making mechanisms to provide liquidity for borrowing and lending activities. Users can contribute their assets to these pools, which are then used to fulfill borrowing requests. Automated market making algorithms ensure efficient borrowing and lending rates based on the available liquidity. Liquidity providers earn a share of the interest generated by the lending protocol, incentivizing participation in the pool.

Decentralized Risk Assessment:

DeFi lending protocols often rely on decentralized risk assessment mechanisms to evaluate borrowers' creditworthiness. Instead of relying solely on traditional credit scoring models, these protocols leverage on-chain data, including borrowers' collateral and transaction history, to assess risk. This decentralized risk assessment enables greater access to credit for individuals who may not have a traditional credit history, opening up opportunities for underserved markets.

Lending and borrowing protocols in DeFi empower individuals by enabling access to credit and passive income generation. Through smart contracts and collateralized loans, these protocols foster peer-to-peer lending, reduce reliance on intermediaries, and create transparent and efficient credit markets. With interest rates, overcollateralization, and decentralized risk assessment, DeFi lending protocols offer new avenues for financial inclusion and empowerment within the decentralized finance ecosystem.

YIELD FARMING: MAXIMIZING RETURNS IN DEFI

Yield farming has emerged as a popular practice within the DeFi ecosystem, offering participants the opportunity to earn high returns on their cryptocurrency holdings. By leveraging various decentralized finance protocols and strategies, yield farming allows individuals to optimize their capital deployment and generate passive income. Let's explore the key components and functionalities of yield farming in DeFi.

Liquidity Provision:

At the heart of yield farming is liquidity provision. Participants provide liquidity by depositing their assets into liquidity pools or liquidity mining programs. These pools are used by decentralized exchanges, lending protocols, or other DeFi platforms to facilitate transactions or provide liquidity for various financial activities. Liquidity providers are rewarded with yield in the form of fees, interest, or governance tokens, depending on the specific protocol.

Automated Market Making (AMM):

Many yield farming strategies are based on automated market making (AMM) algorithms. These algorithms facilitate decentralized trading by determining asset prices and executing trades based on predefined mathematical formulas. AMM models, often utilized by decentralized exchanges (DEXs), balance the supply and demand of assets within liquidity pools, enabling efficient and continuous trading. Yield farmers contribute assets to these pools and earn a share of the trading fees generated.

Yield Optimization Strategies:

Yield farming involves implementing various strategies to maximize returns. Participants may employ different techniques, such as yield aggregators, yield optimization platforms, or token swapping mechanisms, to allocate their assets efficiently. These strategies aim to identify the most profitable opportunities, including those with the highest yields or incentives, across different DeFi protocols.

Staking and Governance Participation

Staking is another common practice in yield farming. By staking their tokens, individuals contribute to the security and operation of blockchain networks, such as proof-of-stake (PoS) networks. In return, stakers receive rewards, typically in the form of additional tokens, for their contribution. Yield farmers often stake their tokens to earn staking rewards and may participate in governance by voting on protocol upgrades, fee structures, or other important decisions.

Risk Assessment and Mitigation:

Yield farming involves assessing and mitigating risks associated with different protocols and strategies. Participants must evaluate factors such as smart contract security, protocol audits, historical performance, and market conditions. Due diligence is essential to mitigate potential risks, including impermanent loss, smart contract vulnerabilities, or protocol failures. Diversification and careful asset allocation are also key risk management strategies in yield farming.

Tokenomics and Incentives:

Tokenomics and incentives play a crucial role in yield farming. Many protocols introduce their native governance tokens or reward users with additional tokens to incentivize participation. These tokens often have utility within the ecosystem, providing governance rights, fee discounts, or other benefits. Participants can leverage these incentives to enhance their overall yield farming strategies.

Yield farming enables participants to optimize their capital utilization and generate passive income in the DeFi space. By providing liquidity, utilizing automated market making algorithms, and implementing various yield optimization strategies, individuals can access attractive returns on their cryptocurrency holdings. However, it is important to note that yield farming carries risks, including smart contract vulnerabilities, impermanent loss, or changes in market dynamics. Thorough research, risk assessment, and an understanding of the protocols and strategies involved are crucial to successful and secure yield farming practices within the decentralized finance ecosystem.

BENEFITS AND ADVANTAGES OF DEFI: EMPOWERING FINANCIAL FREEDOM

Decentralized Finance (DeFi) has rapidly gained popularity and attention for its transformative potential in the financial landscape. By leveraging blockchain technology and smart contracts, DeFi offers numerous benefits and advantages over traditional financial systems. Let's explore some of the key advantages of DeFi in empowering individuals and reshaping the future of finance.

Financial Inclusivity:

DeFi brings financial services to individuals who are traditionally underserved by the banking system. With a smartphone and an internet connection, anyone can access DeFi platforms and participate in various financial activities, regardless of their geographic location or socio-economic background. DeFi promotes financial inclusivity by providing equal opportunities for individuals to save, invest, borrow, and participate in the global economy.

Open and Transparent:

One of the fundamental principles of DeFi is transparency. Transactions and activities within the decentralized finance ecosystem are recorded on public blockchains, allowing for real-time auditing and verification. This transparency builds trust among participants, as it ensures that financial operations are conducted in a fair and accountable manner. Users can verify the integrity of transactions and have visibility into the underlying smart contracts, fostering a sense of security and confidence.

Elimination of Intermediaries:

DeFi removes the need for traditional intermediaries such as banks, brokers, or clearinghouses. By utilizing smart contracts and decentralized protocols, individuals can directly interact with the DeFi ecosystem. This eliminates the dependency on intermediaries, reducing costs, minimizing the potential for human error or fraud, and increasing the efficiency of financial transactions. DeFi empowers individuals to have full control over their assets, enabling self-custody and removing the risk of funds being held by third parties.

Programmable Money and Automation:

DeFi introduces programmability to money and financial transactions. Smart contracts enable the automation and customization of financial operations, allowing for the creation of complex protocols and applications. DeFi platforms provide a programmable infrastructure where developers can build and deploy innovative financial products, such as decentralized exchanges, lending platforms, yield farming protocols, and more. The programmability of DeFi opens up endless possibilities for creating new financial instruments and services.

Enhanced Access to Liquidity:

DeFi offers improved liquidity options compared to traditional finance. Liquidity pools, decentralized exchanges, and lending protocols enable individuals to access liquidity quickly and efficiently. Users can participate in decentralized lending and borrowing, trade digital assets, provide liquidity to earn passive income, and access diverse financial markets 24/7. DeFi eliminates the geographical and time restrictions associated with traditional financial systems, providing greater accessibility to global markets.

Innovation and Experimentation:

DeFi fosters a culture of innovation and experimentation. With open-source code and permissionless innovation, anyone can contribute to the development of DeFi protocols and applications. This collaborative approach leads to a rapid pace of innovation, with new projects, features, and improvements continuously emerging. DeFi's open nature encourages experimentation and creativity, allowing for the exploration of new financial models and the potential to redefine the future of finance.

Financial Empowerment and Ownership:

Perhaps one of the most significant advantages of DeFi is the empowerment it offers to individuals. By enabling direct control over financial assets and activities, DeFi puts individuals in charge of their financial destiny. Participants can make autonomous decisions regarding savings, investments, and borrowing, without relying on intermediaries. DeFi promotes financial sovereignty, allowing individuals to have ownership and control over their wealth, and fosters a more inclusive and equitable financial system.

These benefits and advantages demonstrate the potential of DeFi to reshape the financial landscape and empower individuals worldwide. With its focus on inclusivity, transparency, efficiency, and innovation, DeFi provides an opportunity for individuals to participate actively in the global financial ecosystem, unlocking new avenues for financial freedom, growth, and prosperity.

RISKS AND CHALLENGES IN DEFI: NAVIGATING THE DECENTRALIZED LANDSCAPE

While Decentralized Finance (DeFi) offers numerous benefits and opportunities, it is essential to recognize and understand the risks and challenges associated with this rapidly evolving ecosystem. As with any financial system, DeFi carries certain inherent risks that participants should be aware of. Let's explore some of the key risks and challenges in DeFi.

Smart Contract Vulnerabilities:

Smart contracts are the backbone of many DeFi protocols. However, they can be susceptible to vulnerabilities or coding errors, which may be exploited by malicious actors. These vulnerabilities can lead to financial losses or security breaches. It is crucial for participants to conduct thorough audits, review smart contract code, and exercise caution when interacting with new or untested protocols. The use of audited and well-established protocols can mitigate the risks associated with smart contract vulnerabilities.

Market Volatility and Price Risk:

The cryptocurrency market is known for its volatility. Price fluctuations can significantly impact the value of assets held within DeFi protocols. Sudden market downturns or extreme price swings can result in substantial losses for participants. It is important to consider the potential risks associated with market volatility and make informed decisions based on individual risk tolerance and investment strategies.

Impermanent Loss:

Impermanent loss is a specific risk for liquidity providers in decentralized exchanges and liquidity pools. When providing liquidity, the value of the deposited assets may change relative to each other over time. This can result in a temporary loss of value compared to holding the assets outside the liquidity pool. Liquidity providers should carefully assess the potential impermanent loss and consider the long-term benefits and rewards of providing liquidity.

Regulatory Uncertainty:

DeFi operates in a rapidly evolving regulatory landscape. Different jurisdictions have varying approaches to cryptocurrency and decentralized finance. Regulatory changes or actions can have an impact on the availability, legality, or operation of DeFi protocols. Participants should stay informed about regulatory developments, comply with applicable laws, and exercise caution when engaging in activities that may be subject to regulatory scrutiny.

Centralization Risks:

While DeFi aims to eliminate centralized intermediaries, certain aspects of the ecosystem may still exhibit centralization risks. For example, liquidity concentration in a few key protocols or large token holders exerting significant influence can introduce systemic risks. Participants should be aware of such risks and diversify their exposure across different platforms and protocols to minimize the potential impact of centralization risks.

User Error and Security:

DeFi platforms often require users to manage their private keys and interact directly with smart contracts. User error, such as incorrectly entering addresses or losing access to private keys, can lead to irreversible loss of funds. It is essential to exercise caution, implement robust security measures, and use reputable wallet solutions to safeguard assets and prevent unauthorized access.

Scalability and Network Congestion:

As DeFi gains popularity, network congestion on certain blockchains, such as Ethereum, can increase. High transaction fees and network congestion can limit accessibility and impact the user experience. Scaling solutions and the development of layer 2 protocols are being explored to address these challenges, but participants should be aware of potential limitations and plan accordingly.

Navigating the risks and challenges in DeFi requires a proactive and informed approach. Participants should conduct thorough research, exercise due diligence, and carefully assess the risks and rewards of engaging with specific protocols or activities. Staying updated with the latest developments, maintaining security best practices, and diversifying investments can contribute to a more secure and resilient DeFi experience.

GETTING STARTED WITH DEFI: SETTING UP A DIGITAL WALLET

To embark on your journey in the world of Decentralized Finance (DeFi), the first step is to set up a digital wallet. A digital wallet, also known as a cryptocurrency wallet, enables you to securely store, send, and receive digital assets such as cryptocurrencies. Here's a guide to help you get started:

Choose a Digital Wallet:

There are different types of digital wallets available, including web wallets, mobile wallets, desktop wallets, and hardware wallets. Each has its advantages and considerations. Web wallets are convenient as they can be accessed through a web browser, but they may be less secure compared to other options. Mobile wallets provide flexibility, allowing you to manage your assets on the go. Desktop wallets offer increased security by storing your assets locally on your computer. Hardware wallets are physical devices that offer the highest level of security by storing your assets offline. Consider your preferences and security requirements when selecting a wallet.

Research Wallet Providers:

Once you've determined the type of wallet you prefer, research different wallet providers to find a reputable and reliable option. Look for well-established providers with positive user reviews and a track record of security. Consider factors such as ease of use, supported cryptocurrencies, backup and recovery options, and additional security features like two-factor authentication (2FA). It's important to choose a wallet that aligns with your needs and provides a seamless user experience.

Download and Install the Wallet:

If you choose a mobile or desktop wallet, visit the official website of your chosen wallet provider to download the wallet application. Ensure that you download from the official source to avoid fake or malicious applications. Follow the installation instructions provided by the wallet provider, and make sure to verify the authenticity of the application before proceeding.

Set Up Your Wallet:

Once the wallet is installed, open the application and follow the on-screen instructions to set up your wallet. This usually involves creating a secure password or PIN and generating a unique recovery phrase or seed phrase. The recovery phrase is a crucial component of wallet security, as it allows you to restore access to your wallet in case of loss or device failure. Write down the recovery phrase and store it in a safe and offline location. Do not share it with anyone or store it electronically, as it could be compromised.

Secure Your Wallet:

Take additional security measures to protect your wallet. Enable two-factor authentication (2FA) if supported by your chosen wallet provider. Consider using a hardware wallet for enhanced security, especially if you plan to hold significant amounts of cryptocurrencies. Keep your wallet software up to date by installing updates and security patches as they become available.

Back Up Your Wallet:

Regularly back up your wallet to ensure that you can recover your funds in case of loss or unforeseen circumstances. Wallets typically offer an option to export your private keys or recovery phrase. Follow the wallet provider's instructions to create a backup and securely store it offline. Make sure to test your backup and ensure that you can restore your wallet successfully using the backup information.

With your digital wallet set up, you are now ready to explore the exciting world of DeFi. Remember to practice caution and conduct thorough research before engaging with any DeFi protocol or investing your assets. As you become more familiar with DeFi, you can start connecting your wallet to decentralized exchanges, lending platforms, and other DeFi services to maximize your financial opportunities and participate in the decentralized finance revolution.

GETTING STARTED WITH DEFI: CHOOSING THE RIGHT DEFI PLATFORMS

Once you have set up your digital wallet, the next step in your journey into Decentralized Finance (DeFi) is to choose the right DeFi platforms to engage with. DeFi offers a wide range of protocols and applications, each with its own features, benefits, and considerations. Here's a guide to help you select the right DeFi platforms for your needs:

Understand Your Goals and Risk Tolerance:

Before diving into DeFi, it's essential to define your goals and understand your risk tolerance. Consider factors such as your investment objectives, desired level of involvement, and the amount of risk you are willing to take. Some individuals may be interested in earning passive income through lending and liquidity provision, while others may seek exposure to specific tokens or investment opportunities. Aligning your goals and risk tolerance will help you make informed decisions when selecting DeFi platforms.

Research DeFi Protocols and Projects:

Explore the DeFi landscape and conduct thorough research on different protocols and projects. Consider factors such as the team behind the project, the protocol's security measures, the level of adoption and community engagement, and the track record of the protocol. Look for projects with a strong reputation, audited smart contracts, and an active community. Read project documentation, whitepapers, and reviews to gain a deeper understanding of the protocol's goals, mechanics, and potential risks.

Consider User Experience and Interface:

Evaluate the user experience and interface of the DeFi platforms you are considering. DeFi platforms vary in terms of user-friendliness, design, and ease of navigation. Look for platforms that provide an intuitive and user-friendly interface, making it easy to navigate and interact with the protocols. Consider platforms that offer clear instructions, tutorials, and customer support to help users navigate their services effectively.

Assess Security Measures:

Security is paramount in the DeFi ecosystem. Assess the security measures implemented by the platforms you are considering. Look for platforms that prioritize security through smart contract audits, bug bounties, and transparency about their security practices. Platforms that offer insurance coverage or collaborations with reputable security auditors can provide additional peace of mind. Choose platforms with a strong track record of security and a commitment to ongoing security improvements.

Evaluate Liquidity and Volume:

Liquidity is a crucial aspect of DeFi platforms, especially if you plan to engage in activities such as trading or providing liquidity. Evaluate the liquidity and trading volume on the platforms you are considering. Higher liquidity and trading volume generally provide better price stability and a more efficient trading experience. Consider platforms that have established themselves as reputable venues for liquidity provision or trading, as they attract a larger user base and offer more opportunities.

Review Tokenomics and Governance:

If a DeFi protocol has its native token or incorporates governance mechanisms, review the tokenomics and governance structure. Understand the utility of the token within the protocol and any incentives or rewards associated with it. Evaluate the governance model, such as voting mechanisms or community involvement, to ensure alignment with your values and interests.

Community and Reputation:

Assess the community and reputation of the DeFi platforms you are considering. Engage with the community by joining forums, social media channels, or attending community events to gain insights into the platform's user experience, responsiveness, and overall reputation. A strong and active community can provide valuable support, knowledge-sharing, and a sense of trust.

Remember, DeFi is a dynamic and rapidly evolving space. Stay informed about the latest developments, news, and updates within the DeFi ecosystem. As you gain more experience and familiarity with different platforms, you can gradually expand your engagement and explore new opportunities. By selecting the right DeFi platforms, you can effectively participate in the decentralized finance revolution and unlock the potential for financial innovation, growth, and empowerment.

GETTING STARTED WITH DEFI: SECURITY BEST PRACTICES

When engaging in Decentralized Finance (DeFi), ensuring the security of your digital assets and personal information is paramount. The decentralized nature of DeFi comes with certain risks, but by following security best practices, you can mitigate potential threats and protect yourself from malicious actors. Here are some essential security measures to consider:

Secure Your Digital Wallet:

Protecting your digital wallet is crucial for safeguarding your assets. Take the following steps to enhance wallet security:
- Use a strong, unique password for your wallet and avoid reusing passwords from other accounts.
- Enable two-factor authentication (2FA) wherever possible to provide an additional layer of security.
- Consider using a hardware wallet, such as a Ledger or Trezor device, which stores your private keys offline and provides enhanced security against online threats.

Verify the Authenticity of Websites and Applications:

To avoid falling victim to phishing attacks or downloading malicious software, always verify the authenticity of websites and applications before providing sensitive information or downloading anything. Be cautious of phishing emails, social media messages, or links that direct you to fake platforms. Double-check URLs, ensure you are visiting official websites, and only download applications from trusted sources.

Be Wary of Suspicious Links and Downloads:

Exercise caution when clicking on links or downloading files related to DeFi. Avoid clicking on links from untrusted sources, and be skeptical of unsolicited messages or advertisements promising extraordinary returns or asking for sensitive information. Malicious links or downloads may lead to the compromise of your wallet or personal information.

Research and Verify DeFi Projects:

Thoroughly research DeFi projects before engaging with them. Look for reputable projects with a strong track record, audited smart contracts, and an active community. Verify the legitimacy of the team and their backgrounds. Read project documentation and user reviews to gain insights into the project's security measures and any potential vulnerabilities.

Stay Informed About Security Vulnerabilities:

Keep yourself updated about security vulnerabilities and best practices within the DeFi ecosystem. Subscribe to reputable security newsletters, follow security-focused blogs or social media accounts, and participate in relevant online communities. Being aware of the latest security risks and countermeasures will help you make informed decisions and protect your assets effectively.

Diversify Your Investments:

Spreading your investments across different DeFi projects can help mitigate risk. By diversifying, you reduce the impact of potential vulnerabilities or losses associated with a single project. However, ensure that you thoroughly research each project and understand its risks and rewards before allocating your assets.

Regularly Update Software and Firmware:

Keep your wallet software, applications, and firmware up to date. Developers regularly release updates that address security vulnerabilities and improve overall performance. Set up automatic updates whenever possible or manually check for updates periodically.

Use Secure Networks and Devices:

When accessing your wallet or engaging with DeFi platforms, use secure networks and devices. Avoid using public Wi-Fi networks, as they can be compromised. Instead, connect to trusted networks or use a virtual private network (VPN) to encrypt your internet connection. Keep your devices secure by using strong passwords, enabling automatic device locking, and regularly updating your operating system and antivirus software.

Be Cautious with Personal Information:

Exercise caution when sharing personal information related to your DeFi activities. Be wary of platforms or individuals that request unnecessary personal data beyond what is required for authentication or compliance purposes. Never share your private keys, recovery phrases, or sensitive information with anyone.

Trust Your Instincts:

Lastly, trust your instincts. If something seems suspicious or too good to be true, take a step back and conduct thorough research. Trustworthy projects and platforms prioritize security and will never ask for your private keys or sensitive information.

By following these security best practices, you can enhance your security posture in the DeFi ecosystem and protect your digital assets. Stay vigilant, stay informed, and be proactive in safeguarding your wallet, personal information, and overall digital presence.

EXPLORING DEFI USE CASES: DECENTRALIZED LENDING AND BORROWING

Decentralized Finance (DeFi) has revolutionized the lending and borrowing landscape, providing individuals with unprecedented opportunities to access credit and earn interest on their digital assets. By leveraging blockchain technology and smart contracts, DeFi lending and borrowing protocols offer numerous benefits over traditional financial systems. Let's dive into the use cases and advantages of decentralized lending and borrowing within the DeFi ecosystem:

Peer-to-Peer Lending:

DeFi lending protocols enable individuals to engage in peer-to-peer lending without the need for intermediaries. Borrowers can obtain loans by collateralizing their digital assets, such as cryptocurrencies, while lenders can provide liquidity and earn interest on their holdings. This peer-to-peer lending model eliminates the reliance on banks or other financial institutions, promoting greater accessibility, reduced bureaucracy, and potentially lower interest rates.

Global Accessibility:

Decentralized lending and borrowing platforms operate on blockchain networks, allowing participants to access credit and provide liquidity from anywhere in the world. This global accessibility breaks down geographic barriers and expands financial opportunities for individuals who may not have access to traditional banking systems. All that is needed is an internet connection and a digital wallet, enabling individuals to participate in the DeFi lending ecosystem regardless of their location.

Collateralized Loans:

DeFi lending platforms commonly utilize collateralized loans, where borrowers lock their digital assets as collateral to secure loans. Collateralization mitigates the risk for lenders, as they have recourse in the event of default. The value of the collateral is typically higher than the borrowed amount, reducing the risk of non-payment and increasing the chances of loan recovery. Collateralized loans in DeFi provide a secure and efficient mechanism for borrowers to access credit while protecting lenders' interests.

Lower Barriers to Entry:

Decentralized lending platforms have lower barriers to entry compared to traditional lending systems. In many cases, users can borrow and lend with minimal account setup, credit checks, or extensive paperwork. This inclusivity enables individuals who may not have a traditional credit history or access to banking services to participate in lending and borrowing activities. DeFi lending democratizes access to credit, promoting financial inclusivity and empowering individuals worldwide.

Smart contracts power DeFi lending protocols, enabling automated and transparent lending and borrowing processes. Loan terms, interest rates, and collateral requirements are predefined in the smart contract code and executed automatically. This automation eliminates the need for intermediaries, reduces human error, and ensures the immutability and transparency of loan agreements. Participants can trust that the terms of the loan will be enforced as programmed, fostering a trustless and efficient lending environment.

Earn Passive Income:

Lenders in DeFi lending platforms have the opportunity to earn passive income by providing liquidity and earning interest on their digital assets. Instead of leaving assets idle, individuals can deploy their holdings in lending protocols and earn a return on their investment. Lending platforms often provide competitive interest rates compared to traditional savings accounts, offering an attractive option for individuals looking to earn passive income on their digital assets.

Diverse Loan Types:

DeFi lending protocols support various loan types beyond simple borrowing and lending. Platforms may offer features such as flash loans, which allow borrowers to access funds without collateral, provided they repay the loan within a single transaction. Others provide functionality for margin trading, enabling users to amplify their trading positions with borrowed funds. These diverse loan types offer advanced financial opportunities and strategies within the DeFi lending ecosystem.

Decentralized lending and borrowing in DeFi have transformed the way individuals access credit and earn interest on their digital assets. By leveraging the power of blockchain technology, smart contracts, and peer-to-peer transactions, DeFi lending protocols promote financial inclusivity, global accessibility, and automated processes. As the DeFi ecosystem continues to innovate, lending and borrowing protocols will play a crucial role in reshaping the future of finance, providing individuals with more control, transparency, and opportunities within the decentralized financial landscape.

EXPLORING DEFI USE CASES: AUTOMATED MARKET MAKING

Automated Market Making (AMM) is a key component of Decentralized Finance (DeFi) that has revolutionized the way digital assets are traded. AMM algorithms facilitate efficient and continuous trading by determining asset prices based on predefined mathematical formulas. Let's explore the use cases and advantages of automated market making within the DeFi ecosystem:

Liquidity Provision:

One of the primary use cases of automated market making is providing liquidity to decentralized exchanges (DEXs) and other DeFi platforms. Liquidity providers lock their assets into liquidity pools, which are utilized for trading purposes. By providing liquidity, individuals contribute to the overall trading volume and depth of the market, making it easier for traders to buy or sell assets without significant price slippage. Automated market making enables the continuous availability of liquidity, improving market efficiency and user experience.

Efficient Price Determination:

AMM algorithms automatically determine asset prices based on mathematical formulas, such as the constant product formula (used in popular AMMs like Uniswap). These formulas ensure that trades are executed at fair prices based on the ratio of assets in the liquidity pool. As trade volume and liquidity change, AMM algorithms automatically adjust prices to maintain equilibrium, reducing the impact of large buy or sell orders on asset prices. This efficient price determination mechanism enables traders to access fair and competitive prices for their transactions.

Decentralized Exchange Functionality:

Automated market making is a fundamental component of decentralized exchanges (DEXs). DEXs leverage AMM algorithms to enable users to trade digital assets directly from their wallets without the need for intermediaries or centralized order books. AMMs power the swapping functionality of DEXs, ensuring continuous liquidity and allowing users to trade assets instantly at prevailing market prices. This decentralized exchange functionality promotes transparency, eliminates counterparty risk, and gives individuals full control over their assets.

Incentivizing Liquidity Provision:

AMMs incentivize liquidity provision by rewarding liquidity providers with transaction fees or governance tokens. Liquidity providers earn a share of the trading fees generated within the liquidity pool based on their proportional contribution. In some cases, liquidity providers also receive governance tokens, which enable participation in the decision-making process of the protocol. These incentives encourage individuals to provide liquidity, creating a vibrant and self-sustaining ecosystem of liquidity provision.

Diverse Trading Opportunities:

AMMs open up diverse trading opportunities within the DeFi ecosystem. Traders can access a wide range of assets and trade pairs that may not be available on traditional exchanges. With the composability of DeFi protocols, traders can seamlessly interact with multiple AMMs, allowing for complex trading strategies and access to a broader range of markets. AMMs enable traders to speculate, hedge positions, and actively manage their digital asset portfolios in a decentralized and permissionless manner.

Accessibility and Global Participation:

Automated market making in DeFi promotes accessibility and global participation in trading activities. DeFi protocols operate on blockchain networks, allowing users from anywhere in the world to engage in trading without the need for intermediaries or geographical restrictions. Individuals can trade 24/7, enabling participation in global markets and bridging the gap between different financial ecosystems. AMMs democratize access to trading, providing individuals with the opportunity to participate in the global financial landscape regardless of their location.

Innovation and Token Launches:

AMMs have also facilitated innovation in the launch and distribution of new tokens. Initial DEX Offerings (IDOs) allow projects to launch their tokens directly on DEXs, leveraging AMM algorithms for price discovery and liquidity provision. This opens up opportunities for new projects to raise capital, engage with their communities, and bootstrap liquidity in a decentralized and inclusive manner. AMMs enable efficient token launches and offer investors early access to new investment opportunities.

Automated market making plays a vital role in the DeFi ecosystem by providing continuous liquidity, efficient price determination, and enabling decentralized exchange functionality. AMMs incentivize liquidity provision, creating vibrant trading environments with diverse opportunities for users. As DeFi continues to evolve, automated market making will remain a core component, fostering innovation, liquidity, and accessibility in the decentralized financial landscape.

EXPLORING DEFI USE CASES: YIELD FARMING AND STAKING

Yield farming and staking are prominent use cases within the Decentralized Finance (DeFi) ecosystem that enable individuals to maximize returns on their digital assets while actively participating in the growth and governance of decentralized protocols. These use cases provide opportunities for individuals to earn rewards, contribute to the network's security, and shape the future of decentralized finance. Let's explore the use cases and advantages of yield farming and staking within DeFi:

Earning Passive Income:

Yield farming and staking offer the opportunity to earn passive income on digital assets. By providing liquidity to DeFi protocols, users can earn rewards in the form of additional tokens, transaction fees, or interest on their holdings. Stakers, on the other hand, can lock their assets to secure a network and earn staking rewards. These mechanisms allow individuals to earn returns on their assets while holding them, making them an attractive option for those seeking to generate passive income in the decentralized financial ecosystem.

Liquidity Provision and Market Efficiency:

Yield farming involves providing liquidity to decentralized exchanges (DEXs), lending protocols, or liquidity pools. By contributing liquidity, individuals enhance market efficiency, reduce slippage, and improve the overall user experience for traders. Yield farming incentivizes individuals to supply liquidity by rewarding them with protocol-specific tokens or a share of transaction fees. This process creates a symbiotic relationship where liquidity providers earn rewards while enabling the smooth functioning of DeFi markets.

Participating in Governance:

Staking is often associated with governance tokens that grant holders the ability to participate in the decision-making process of a protocol. By staking their tokens, individuals can actively contribute to the governance of decentralized platforms, including voting on proposals, proposing changes, or participating in community discussions. Staking empowers users to shape the direction and development of DeFi protocols, providing a voice in the evolution of the ecosystem.

Network Security:

Staking plays a vital role in securing decentralized networks. By staking their tokens, individuals contribute to the consensus mechanism of a blockchain, such as proof-of-stake (PoS). Stakers help validate transactions, secure the network against potential attacks, and maintain the integrity of the blockchain. In return for their contribution, stakers earn rewards, incentivizing them to actively participate in securing and maintaining the decentralized infrastructure.

Access to New Token Offerings:

Yield farming and staking provide early access to new token offerings and investment opportunities within the DeFi ecosystem. Projects often distribute their tokens through liquidity mining programs or token incentives for staking. This allows participants to be part of a project's growth from its early stages and potentially benefit from the appreciation of the token's value over time.

Diversification and Risk Management:

Yield farming and staking enable individuals to diversify their digital asset holdings and manage risk. By allocating assets to different protocols or liquidity pools, individuals can spread their risk across multiple platforms and strategies. This diversification helps mitigate potential losses in the event of unforeseen events or vulnerabilities in a particular protocol.

Educational and Learning Opportunities:

Yield farming and staking provide educational opportunities for individuals to learn about various DeFi protocols and financial instruments. Engaging in these activities encourages participants to understand the mechanics, risks, and potential rewards associated with different strategies. Yield farmers and stakers gain valuable insights into the DeFi landscape, deepen their understanding of decentralized finance, and develop new skills in managing their digital assets.

Yield farming and staking have transformed the way individuals engage with their digital assets in the DeFi ecosystem. By participating in these activities, individuals can earn passive income, contribute to network security and governance, access new investment opportunities, and diversify their holdings. These use cases have fueled the growth and innovation of decentralized finance, providing individuals with opportunities for active participation, financial growth, and shaping the future of the decentralized financial landscape.

EXPLORING DEFI USE CASES: TOKEN SWAPPING AND LIQUIDITY PROVISION

Token swapping and liquidity provision are fundamental use cases within the Decentralized Finance (DeFi) ecosystem that facilitate seamless asset exchange and enable individuals to provide liquidity to decentralized exchanges (DEXs) and other DeFi platforms. These use cases empower users to efficiently trade digital assets and contribute to the liquidity and overall functionality of decentralized markets. Let's delve into the advantages and use cases of token swapping and liquidity provision in DeFi:

Efficient Asset Exchange:

Token swapping allows users to exchange one digital asset for another directly on decentralized exchanges without the need for intermediaries or centralized order books. Decentralized exchanges leverage automated market making (AMM) algorithms to determine asset prices and execute trades. This efficient asset exchange mechanism provides users with instant access to a wide range of digital assets at prevailing market prices, reducing the need for multiple steps or intermediaries involved in traditional exchanges.

Decentralized Exchange Functionality:

Token swapping plays a central role in the functionality of decentralized exchanges (DEXs). DEXs enable users to trade digital assets directly from their wallets, without having to deposit funds into a centralized exchange or rely on third-party custodians. Token swapping ensures continuous liquidity within DEXs, allowing users to buy and sell assets instantly at fair market prices. Decentralized exchanges promote transparency, eliminate counterparty risk, and provide users with greater control over their assets.

Increased Market Accessibility:

Token swapping and decentralized exchanges increase market accessibility for individuals worldwide. Users can access a broad range of digital assets and trade pairs that may not be available on traditional exchanges. The decentralized nature of token swapping ensures that users can trade 24/7, transcending geographical boundaries and eliminating the limitations imposed by traditional banking hours or trading sessions. This accessibility empowers individuals to participate in global markets and seize investment opportunities from anywhere in the world.

Liquidity Provision:

Liquidity provision is a crucial use case within DeFi facilitated by token swapping. Users can provide liquidity to liquidity pools, which are utilized for trading purposes on decentralized exchanges and other DeFi platforms. By contributing liquidity, individuals enhance market depth and stability, reducing price slippage and improving trading experiences. Liquidity provision incentivizes individuals to allocate their digital assets to these pools by rewarding them with transaction fees or protocol-specific tokens.

Earning Rewards:

Liquidity providers in decentralized exchanges or liquidity pools earn rewards for their contributions. These rewards can take the form of additional tokens, transaction fees, or governance tokens, depending on the platform. By providing liquidity, individuals can earn a passive income on their digital assets while helping to maintain market efficiency and liquidity. This rewards-based model encourages participation and incentivizes individuals to actively engage in liquidity provision activities.

Diverse Trading Opportunities:

Token swapping and liquidity provision enable diverse trading opportunities within the DeFi ecosystem. Users can trade a wide range of digital assets and access various trading pairs that may not be available on traditional exchanges. The composability of DeFi protocols allows users to seamlessly interact with multiple decentralized exchanges, enabling advanced trading strategies and access to a broader range of markets. Token swapping and liquidity provision empower users to actively manage their digital asset portfolios and explore diverse investment opportunities.

Innovation in Token Distribution:

Token swapping and liquidity provision have paved the way for innovative token distribution mechanisms. Initial DEX Offerings (IDOs) allow projects to distribute their tokens directly on decentralized exchanges, leveraging the liquidity and token swapping functionality. This approach provides users with early access to new tokens and investment opportunities, while allowing projects to bootstrap liquidity and engage with their communities in a decentralized and inclusive manner.

Token swapping and liquidity provision have transformed the way individuals trade digital assets and contribute to the liquidity of decentralized markets. These use cases provide efficient asset exchange, increase market accessibility, and enable users to earn rewards for liquidity provision. By participating in token swapping and providing liquidity, individuals actively contribute to the growth and functionality of the DeFi ecosystem, shaping the future of decentralized finance.

EXPLORING DEFI USE CASES IN VARIOUS INDUSTRIES

Decentralized Finance (DeFi) has expanded beyond its initial applications in lending, borrowing, and liquidity provision. The versatility of DeFi protocols and blockchain technology has enabled innovative use cases across multiple industries. Let's explore how DeFi is being applied in various sectors, including NFTs, gaming, medical, law, business, real estate, education, and more:

Non-Fungible Tokens (NFTs):

DeFi has intersected with the booming NFT market, enabling fractional ownership, decentralized marketplaces, and lending platforms for NFT assets. NFTs represent unique digital assets, such as artwork, collectibles, or virtual real estate. DeFi protocols provide liquidity to NFT owners, allowing them to unlock the value of their assets without needing to sell them entirely. NFT-backed loans and fractional ownership allow investors to diversify their holdings and participate in the NFT market.

Gaming:

DeFi and blockchain technology are transforming the gaming industry by introducing decentralized ownership, provable scarcity, and interoperability of in-game assets. Gamers can own and trade virtual assets securely using blockchain-based gaming platforms. DeFi protocols enable the creation of decentralized marketplaces, where players can buy, sell, and lend their virtual assets. Additionally, DeFi gaming platforms provide mechanisms for rewarding players with tokens, enhancing the play-to-earn model.

Medical and Healthcare:

DeFi is making strides in the medical and healthcare sectors, facilitating secure and transparent management of medical records, patient consent, and supply chain tracking. Blockchain-based systems enable patients to have control over their medical data, granting selective access to healthcare providers while maintaining privacy. DeFi solutions can also streamline medical supply chains, ensuring the authenticity and traceability of pharmaceuticals and medical devices, reducing counterfeiting and enhancing patient safety.

Law and Legal Contracts:

DeFi offers possibilities for automating and executing legal contracts using smart contracts. By leveraging self-executing code, DeFi platforms enable the creation of decentralized legal agreements, simplifying and streamlining the contract management process. DeFi also provides opportunities for escrow services, dispute resolution mechanisms, and decentralized governance models within legal frameworks, enhancing transparency and efficiency.

Business and Enterprise Solutions:

DeFi provides solutions for businesses, including decentralized identity management, supply chain financing, and peer-to-peer lending for small and medium enterprises (SMEs). Blockchain-based identity systems enable businesses to manage user identities securely, reducing the risk of data breaches. DeFi lending protocols offer accessible and transparent financing options to SMEs, bypassing traditional financial institutions and enabling direct borrowing from the community.

Real Estate:

DeFi is revolutionizing the real estate industry by introducing fractional ownership, tokenization of properties, and decentralized property rental and management platforms. Real estate assets can be tokenized, enabling investors to buy fractional shares, democratizing access to real estate investments. DeFi platforms facilitate peer-to-peer property rental agreements and transparent management of property-related transactions, reducing intermediaries and increasing efficiency.

Education:

DeFi is disrupting the education sector by enabling secure verification of academic credentials, facilitating micro-credentialing, and incentivizing lifelong learning. Blockchain-based systems can store and verify educational records, ensuring the authenticity of certifications and degrees. DeFi platforms also incentivize learners to acquire new skills and knowledge by rewarding them with tokens or other incentives, promoting continuous learning and upskilling.

These are just a few examples of how DeFi is expanding into various industries, demonstrating the potential of blockchain technology beyond traditional finance. As DeFi continues to evolve, it will likely find applications in many more sectors, driving innovation, transparency, and efficiency in numerous aspects of our daily lives. The intersection of DeFi with different industries holds the promise of transforming traditional systems, empowering individuals, and fostering a more decentralized and inclusive global economy.

DIVING DEEPER: ADVANCED DEFI CONCEPTS - LAYER 2 SCALING SOLUTIONS

As the popularity of Decentralized Finance (DeFi) continues to grow, scalability has become a critical challenge. To address this issue, advanced concepts such as Layer 2 scaling solutions have emerged. Layer 2 solutions aim to enhance the scalability and efficiency of blockchain networks, allowing DeFi platforms to process a higher volume of transactions while reducing congestion and gas fees. Let's dive deeper into Layer 2 scaling solutions in the DeFi ecosystem:

What are Layer 2 Scaling Solutions?

Layer 2 scaling solutions are protocols or techniques that operate on top of existing blockchain networks, enabling increased transaction throughput and reducing the burden on the main blockchain. These solutions aim to alleviate network congestion and high fees by moving some of the transaction processing off-chain while ensuring the security and trustlessness of the system. Layer 2 solutions can enhance the performance of DeFi applications, providing a more seamless and cost-effective user experience.

Types of Layer 2 Scaling Solutions:

There are various types of Layer 2 scaling solutions, including:

State Channels:

State channels enable off-chain transactions between multiple parties while ensuring the final settlement is securely recorded on the blockchain. Users can conduct multiple transactions without incurring the costs and delays associated with on-chain transactions. State channels are well-suited for frequent and fast interactions, such as microtransactions or gaming applications.

Sidechains:

Sidechains are separate blockchain networks that operate parallel to the main blockchain. They can process transactions independently, allowing for increased scalability. Sidechains typically have their consensus mechanisms but maintain a connection to the main blockchain, enabling users to move assets between the main chain and the sidechain.

Plasma:

Plasma is a Layer 2 framework that creates child chains connected to the main blockchain. Child chains can process transactions more quickly and at a lower cost than the main chain. Plasma chains leverage smart contracts and periodically submit transaction data to the main chain for final settlement. Plasma provides scalability while maintaining the security and trustlessness of the main chain.

Rollups:

Rollups are Layer 2 solutions that bundle multiple transactions into a single transaction that is then submitted to the main blockchain. There are two types of rollups:

Optimistic Rollups:

Optimistic Rollups assume that transactions are valid by default, processing them off-chain and submitting a cryptographic proof to the main chain for verification. This approach improves scalability by reducing the amount of data that needs to be processed on the main chain.

Zero-Knowledge (ZK) Rollups:

ZK Rollups use zero-knowledge proofs to validate transactions off-chain while providing succinct proofs of their validity on the main chain. This approach offers increased scalability while maintaining privacy and security.

Benefits of Layer 2 Scaling Solutions:

Layer 2 scaling solutions provide several benefits for the DeFi ecosystem:

Scalability:

Layer 2 solutions significantly increase transaction throughput, enabling DeFi platforms to handle a larger volume of transactions and users without congesting the main blockchain.

Lower Costs:

By moving some transaction processing off-chain, Layer 2 solutions reduce gas fees and transaction costs, making DeFi more accessible and affordable for users.

Improved User Experience:

With faster transaction confirmations and lower fees, Layer 2 solutions enhance the user experience, enabling seamless interactions and reducing the frustration associated with network congestion.

Security and Trustlessness:

Layer 2 solutions maintain the security and trustlessness of the underlying blockchain by leveraging cryptographic proofs, smart contracts, and periodic settlements on the main chain.

Integration with DeFi Applications:

To leverage Layer 2 scaling solutions, DeFi applications need to integrate with compatible protocols or platforms. Many popular DeFi protocols are exploring or implementing Layer 2 solutions to enhance their scalability. By integrating with Layer 2 solutions, DeFi platforms can offer users a more efficient and cost-effective experience, while also expanding the capabilities and potential of their applications.

Adoption Challenges:

While Layer 2 scaling solutions offer significant benefits, widespread adoption faces challenges such as interoperability, security audits, and user awareness. Interoperability between different Layer 2 solutions and compatibility with various DeFi protocols are essential for a seamless user experience. Rigorous security audits and testing are critical to ensure the robustness and reliability of Layer 2 solutions. Additionally, educating users about the advantages and processes of Layer 2 scaling is essential for broader adoption and usage.

Layer 2 scaling solutions are an exciting advancement in the DeFi ecosystem, addressing scalability concerns and improving the overall efficiency and accessibility of decentralized applications. As more projects and protocols adopt Layer 2 solutions, we can expect DeFi to scale to new heights, accommodating a growing user base and enabling a wider range of innovative financial applications on blockchain networks.

DIVING DEEPER: ADVANCED DEFI CONCEPTS - INTEROPERABILITY AND CROSS-CHAIN PROTOCOLS

As the Decentralized Finance (DeFi) ecosystem expands, the need for interoperability and cross-chain protocols becomes increasingly important. Interoperability refers to the ability of different blockchain networks to communicate and interact seamlessly with one another, enabling the transfer of assets and data across multiple chains. Cross-chain protocols facilitate interoperability by establishing bridges between disparate blockchains, allowing users to access a broader range of DeFi applications and assets. Let's explore the concepts of interoperability and cross-chain protocols in the context of advanced DeFi concepts:

What is Interoperability in DeFi?

Interoperability in DeFi refers to the ability of different blockchain networks, each with its own protocols and smart contracts, to communicate and exchange information in a seamless and secure manner. Interoperability enables the transfer of assets, data, and value between different blockchains, expanding the functionality and possibilities of decentralized applications. With interoperability, users can leverage the strengths of multiple blockchain networks and access a broader range of DeFi protocols and services.

The Importance of Interoperability:

Interoperability is crucial for the growth and adoption of the DeFi ecosystem. It allows users to access and utilize assets and services across different blockchain networks, breaking down the barriers between isolated ecosystems. Interoperability enhances liquidity, as assets can move freely between chains, increasing the efficiency of decentralized exchanges and lending platforms. It also promotes collaboration and innovation by enabling developers to leverage the capabilities of multiple blockchains, fostering cross-chain composability and expanding the range of DeFi applications.

Challenges in Achieving Interoperability:

Achieving interoperability in a decentralized and trustless environment presents technical and design challenges. Different blockchains have varying consensus mechanisms, smart contract languages, and security models, making it complex to establish seamless communication. Standardizing protocols and ensuring secure cross-chain transactions requires extensive research, development, and rigorous testing. Additionally, achieving interoperability while maintaining privacy and security is an ongoing challenge in the DeFi space.

Cross-Chain Protocols:

Cross-chain protocols play a vital role in enabling interoperability between disparate blockchains. These protocols establish bridges or connectors that facilitate the transfer of assets and data between different chains. Some prominent cross-chain protocols include:

a. Atomic Swaps:

Atomic swaps allow users to exchange assets between blockchains without the need for intermediaries. It ensures that the swap is either fully completed or not executed at all, eliminating counterparty risk.

b. Wrapped Tokens:

Wrapped tokens are tokens pegged to the value of an underlying asset, typically from a different blockchain. These wrapped tokens enable the transfer of assets between chains while maintaining a consistent representation of their value.

c. Cross-Chain Bridges:

Cross-chain bridges enable the movement of assets and data between different blockchains by locking the assets on one chain and minting equivalent assets on the target chain. These bridges establish trustless and secure connections between blockchains.

d. Interoperability Protocols:

Interoperability protocols, such as Polkadot and Cosmos, provide frameworks and infrastructures for connecting multiple blockchains into a cohesive network. They facilitate secure communication and data transfer, allowing users to access a broader range of services and assets.

Benefits of Interoperability:

Interoperability offers several benefits for the DeFi ecosystem:

a. Enhanced Liquidity:

Interoperability enables assets to move freely between chains, increasing liquidity and reducing fragmentation across different DeFi platforms.

b. Expanded Market Access:

Users can access a wider range of assets and services from different blockchain networks, fostering cross-chain collaboration and providing more diverse investment opportunities.

c. Improved Scalability:

Interoperability allows DeFi applications to leverage the scalability of different blockchains, reducing congestion and improving transaction throughput.

d. Cross-Chain Composability:

Interoperability promotes cross-chain composability, enabling the integration of various protocols and applications from different chains to create new innovative solutions.

e. Risk Diversification:

Users can diversify their risk exposure by spreading their assets across multiple chains, mitigating the impact of potential vulnerabilities or failures in a single chain.

Future Outlook:

As the DeFi ecosystem continues to evolve, achieving robust interoperability will be crucial for its sustained growth and development. Researchers, developers, and blockchain communities are actively working on advancing cross-chain protocols and standards to enable seamless communication and asset transfer between different blockchains. As interoperability improves, we can expect a more interconnected and efficient DeFi landscape, unlocking new possibilities for users, developers, and the broader financial ecosystem.

Interoperability and cross-chain protocols are paving the way for a more interconnected and efficient DeFi ecosystem. By breaking down barriers between blockchains, users gain access to a broader range of assets, services, and opportunities. As the industry continues to innovate and refine cross-chain technologies, the vision of a truly interconnected and interoperable decentralized financial ecosystem comes closer to reality.

DIVING DEEPER: ADVANCED DEFI CONCEPTS - DECENTRALIZED AUTONOMOUS ORGANIZATIONS (DAOS)

Decentralized Autonomous Organizations (DAOs) are an advanced concept within the Decentralized Finance (DeFi) ecosystem that revolutionizes the way organizations are governed and operated. DAOs are self-governing entities that operate based on predefined rules and smart contracts, enabling decentralized decision-making, collective ownership, and community governance. Let's dive deeper into the concept of DAOs and their significance in the DeFi space:

What is a Decentralized Autonomous Organization (DAO)?

A Decentralized Autonomous Organization (DAO) is a digital organization that operates through smart contracts on a blockchain. DAOs are designed to be autonomous and self-governing, eliminating the need for traditional centralized management and decision-making structures. They allow participants to collectively make decisions, manage funds, and govern the organization based on predefined rules encoded in smart contracts.

Key Components of a DAO:

DAOs consist of the following key components:

a. Smart Contracts:

DAOs utilize smart contracts to define the rules and protocols that govern the organization's operations. These smart contracts contain the logic for decision-making, fund management, and community governance.

b. Token Holders:

DAOs are typically governed by token holders who possess voting rights proportional to the number of tokens they hold. Token holders can participate in decision-making processes, vote on proposals, and shape the direction of the organization.

c. Governance Mechanisms:

DAOs employ various governance mechanisms to enable collective decision-making. This may include voting on proposals, signaling through off-chain discussions, or delegating voting power to representatives. DAOs strive to create inclusive and transparent governance processes that align with the interests of the community.

d. Treasury Management:

DAOs often manage a treasury that holds funds contributed by participants. These funds can be used to finance projects, support development efforts, or fund initiatives aligned with the DAO's goals. The management of the treasury is typically governed by the community through voting or other mechanisms.

Benefits and Advantages of DAOs:

DAOs offer several benefits within the DeFi ecosystem:

a. Decentralization:

DAOs promote decentralization by removing the need for centralized authorities or intermediaries. Decision-making power is distributed among token holders, ensuring a more inclusive and democratic approach to governance.

b. Transparency and Auditability:

DAOs operate on public blockchains, allowing for transparent and auditable transactions and decisions. All actions and changes are recorded on the blockchain, ensuring accountability and reducing the potential for fraud or manipulation.

c. Community Ownership and Participation:

DAOs enable participants to have a stake in the organization, aligning their interests with the success of the project. Token holders can actively participate in decision-making, shaping the organization's future and contributing to its growth.

d. Efficiency and Cost Reduction:

DAOs automate governance processes through smart contracts, reducing the need for intermediaries and streamlining decision-making. This increases efficiency and reduces costs associated with traditional organizational structures.

e. Innovation and Collaboration:

DAOs foster collaboration and innovation by providing a platform for individuals to propose and fund projects aligned with the organization's goals. This allows for decentralized funding, ideation, and execution of initiatives within the DAO ecosystem.

Challenges and Considerations:

While DAOs offer significant advantages, they also come with challenges and considerations:

a. Governance Efficiency:

Ensuring efficient decision-making and avoiding governance gridlock can be a challenge for DAOs with a large and diverse token holder base. Implementing effective governance mechanisms and avoiding concentration of voting power is crucial.

b. Security and Code Audits:

Smart contracts underpinning DAOs need to undergo thorough security audits to mitigate the risk of vulnerabilities or exploits. The immutability of blockchain makes it essential to ensure the solidity of smart contracts from the start.

c. Legal and Regulatory Considerations:

DAOs may face legal and regulatory challenges as they operate in a decentralized and cross-jurisdictional manner. Compliance with relevant regulations and addressing potential legal implications is necessary for broader adoption and acceptance.

d. *User Experience and Education:*

The user experience of interacting with DAOs and participating in governance processes can be complex and require a certain level of technical understanding. Improving the user experience and providing educational resources is crucial for widespread adoption and participation.

Future Outlook:

DAOs are at the forefront of the evolution of organizational structures, providing a framework for decentralized decision-making, community ownership, and transparent governance. As the technology matures, we can expect to see greater integration of DAOs with various DeFi protocols, expanded use cases beyond governance, and further exploration of innovative decentralized organizational models. DAOs have the potential to disrupt traditional organizational structures, empowering individuals and communities to collectively govern and shape the future of decentralized finance.

Decentralized Autonomous Organizations (DAOs) are revolutionizing the way organizations are governed and operated within the DeFi ecosystem. By embracing transparency, community participation, and decentralized decision-making, DAOs provide a framework for a more inclusive, democratic, and efficient organizational structure. As the DeFi space continues to evolve, DAOs will play an integral role in shaping the future of decentralized finance and community-driven initiatives.

DEFI TRENDS AND FUTURE OUTLOOK

The Decentralized Finance (DeFi) ecosystem has experienced tremendous growth and innovation since its inception. As the industry continues to mature, several trends are emerging that shape the future outlook of DeFi. Let's explore some of the key trends and predictions for the future of DeFi:

Institutional Adoption:

Institutional players are increasingly recognizing the potential of DeFi. Traditional financial institutions, asset managers, and even central banks are exploring opportunities to integrate DeFi into their operations. Institutional adoption brings additional liquidity, credibility, and regulatory clarity to the DeFi space, paving the way for mainstream acceptance and further growth.

Regulatory Evolution:

As DeFi gains prominence, regulators worldwide are grappling with how to effectively regulate this rapidly evolving ecosystem. Regulatory frameworks will likely continue to evolve to address concerns around investor protection, AML/KYC compliance, and systemic risks. Striking the right balance between innovation and regulation will be essential for the sustainable growth of DeFi.

Interoperability and Cross-Chain Solutions:

Interoperability will play a vital role in the future of DeFi, allowing seamless interaction and asset transfer across different blockchains. Cross-chain solutions, such as interoperability protocols and bridges, will enable increased liquidity, expand market access, and unlock new opportunities for users. Interoperability will foster collaboration, composability, and innovation within the DeFi ecosystem.

Enhanced Scalability:

Scalability has been a persistent challenge for DeFi platforms, often resulting in network congestion and high fees during periods of high demand. Layer 2 scaling solutions, such as state channels and rollups, will continue to gain traction, offering increased transaction throughput and reduced costs. The adoption of scalable blockchain architectures and advancements in Layer

2 solutions will enhance the scalability of DeFi applications.

Expansion of Use Cases:

DeFi will continue to expand beyond its traditional use cases. We can expect to see increased integration of DeFi in various industries, including gaming, NFTs, supply chain management, and healthcare. DeFi will unlock new opportunities for individuals and businesses, enabling efficient value transfer, asset management, and decentralized applications across multiple sectors.

Improved User Experience:

User experience remains a crucial factor for the mass adoption of DeFi. Efforts to enhance user interfaces, reduce complexity, and improve accessibility will continue. User-friendly wallets, intuitive interfaces, and simplified onboarding processes will make DeFi more accessible to a broader audience, driving increased adoption and engagement.

Privacy-Enhancing Technologies:

Privacy remains an important consideration for DeFi users. Privacy-enhancing technologies, such as zero-knowledge proofs and secure multiparty computation, will gain prominence to protect user data, transactional privacy, and sensitive business information. Balancing privacy with regulatory requirements will be a key challenge to address.

Decentralized Identity and Reputation Systems:

Decentralized identity solutions will gain traction, enabling users to control their personal data and maintain privacy while accessing DeFi services. Reputation systems built on blockchain will help establish trust among participants, enabling efficient on-chain credit scoring and lending.

Sustainable Finance and ESG Initiatives:

The focus on Environmental, Social, and Governance (ESG) considerations will extend to the DeFi space. Sustainable finance initiatives, carbon-neutral protocols, and projects promoting social impact will emerge. DeFi will play a role in creating financial instruments and incentives to support environmentally friendly and socially responsible initiatives.

Global Financial Inclusion:

DeFi has the potential to foster financial inclusion by providing access to financial services for the unbanked and underbanked populations worldwide. DeFi protocols can bridge the gap between traditional banking systems and underserved communities, enabling secure and accessible financial solutions.

The future of DeFi is promising, with continued growth, innovation, and integration with traditional finance. As the industry matures, regulatory clarity, scalability solutions, and improved user experience will drive mainstream adoption. Interoperability, expanded use cases, and sustainability considerations will shape the evolution of DeFi, paving the way for a more inclusive, transparent, and efficient financial ecosystem.

CONCLUSION

The Decentralized Finance (DeFi) ecosystem has ushered in a new era of financial innovation, transforming traditional financial systems and empowering individuals with greater control over their assets and financial activities. Throughout this book, we have explored various aspects of DeFi, from its fundamental principles to advanced concepts and emerging trends.

DeFi has revolutionized financial services by leveraging blockchain technology, smart contracts, and decentralized governance. It has introduced key components such as smart contracts, decentralized exchanges, stablecoins, lending and borrowing protocols, yield farming, and much more. These components have created a decentralized and permissionless financial ecosystem that offers numerous benefits and advantages.

By eliminating intermediaries, reducing costs, and increasing accessibility, DeFi has democratized finance, allowing individuals from all corners of the world to participate in global markets, earn passive income, and access a wide range of financial services. It has provided opportunities for financial inclusion, allowing the unbanked and underbanked populations to access banking services, loans, and investment opportunities.

However, as with any rapidly evolving industry, DeFi also faces challenges. Security vulnerabilities, scalability limitations, regulatory concerns, and user experience hurdles need to be addressed to ensure the long-term sustainability and widespread adoption of DeFi.

Looking to the future, we see promising trends that will shape the evolution of DeFi. Institutional adoption, regulatory evolution, interoperability, enhanced scalability, expanded use cases, improved user experience, privacy-enhancing technologies, decentralized identity, and sustainable finance initiatives are all driving the growth and maturation of the DeFi ecosystem.

As the industry continues to innovate, it is crucial to maintain a balance between innovation and responsible development. Collaboration between stakeholders, including developers, regulators, and users, will be key to navigate the challenges and realize the full potential of DeFi.

In conclusion, DeFi represents a paradigm shift in the financial landscape, enabling individuals to take control of their financial lives, access a broader range of services, and participate in a more inclusive and transparent financial system. The future of DeFi holds immense potential for transforming traditional finance, driving financial inclusion, and shaping the future of global economic systems.

As you embark on your journey in the world of DeFi, remember to stay informed, exercise caution, and continuously learn and adapt to the ever-evolving landscape. Embrace the opportunities that DeFi presents, and be a part of shaping the future of finance.

Welcome to the exciting world of Decentralized Finance

A NOTE ON CRYPTO INVESTMENT: EMBRACE RISK, DYOR, AND JOIN CRYPTO CAVE TELEGRAM FOR SUPPORT

Dear Readers,

As you embark on the exciting journey of exploring the world of cryptocurrencies, I feel compelled to share some crucial advice to ensure your experience remains both rewarding and safe. Cryptocurrency investment holds great potential for financial gains, but it is essential to recognize that it also carries inherent risks. Hence, I implore you to approach this domain with caution, wisdom, and a thorough understanding of the assets you invest in.

1. Embrace Risk:

Crypto investments can be highly volatile, and the market can experience rapid and unpredictable fluctuations. While some cryptocurrencies have seen extraordinary gains, others have faced significant losses. Always remember the principle: "Invest only what you can afford to lose." Never jeopardize your financial security by investing more than you can bear to lose.

2. Do Your Own Research (DYOR):

In the crypto world, knowledge is power. Research each cryptocurrency you consider investing in meticulously. Understand its use case, underlying technology, team, and community. Be cautious of any project promising unrealistic gains or using deceptive marketing tactics. Make informed decisions based on solid research rather than following the crowd blindly.

3. Join Crypto Cave Telegram for Support:
https://bit.ly/joincryptochat

The crypto community is vast and diverse, offering immense knowledge and support to enthusiasts like you. I highly recommend joining reputable online communities, such as "Crypto Cave Telegram," where you can interact with experienced traders, investors, and analysts. These communities can be valuable sources of insights, tips, and guidance, helping you stay informed and make better investment choices.

As you delve into the fascinating realm of cryptocurrencies, remember that it is a rapidly evolving space. Always stay updated, remain open to learning, and be cautious of scams or fraudulent schemes. Additionally, consider using secure storage options for your crypto assets, such as hardware wallets, to protect your investments.

In conclusion, crypto investment can be both exciting and profitable, but it requires diligence, research, and a strong community of like-minded individuals for support. Take calculated risks, stay informed, and remember that your journey in the crypto world is a continuous learning process.

Contact me here*: https://linktr.ee/donatelloinvesting*

Wishing you success and prosperity on your crypto venture!

www.ingramcontent.com/pod-product-compliance
Lightning Source LLC
Chambersburg PA
CBHW060000300526
45794CB00003B/1030